Park City Witness

A COLLECTION OF ESSAYS AND ARTWORK
CELEBRATING OPEN SPACE

2ND EDITION

Summit Land Conservancy
Park City, Utah

© 2012 by Summit Land Conservancy
All rights reserved. This publication may not be reproduced in whole or in part without written permission from the publisher and the individual writer or artist responsible for the piece.

P.O. Box 1775
Park City, UT 84060
435-649-9884
www.summitlandconservancy.org

Edited by Jane Gendron
J Gendron Communications
www.jgendron.com

Designed by Liz Craig Myers
Nine-Grain Design
www.nine-grain-design.com

Artwork selected by Megan W. Fernandez

Printed in the United States of America
by TurnKey Direct, Inc.

ISBN-13: 978-0-615-64592-6

ii

Table of Contents: *Essays*

Foreword	*by Jane Gendron*	v
Introduction: Demonology	*by Cheryl Fox*	1
I love this place. This place does not love me back.	*by Joe Totten*	5
Nowhere Elks	*by Chris Waddell*	8
Grounding	*by Kristen Gould Case*	13
Galligan's Bowl	*by Karri Dell Hays*	16
Mending Fences	*by Tom Clyde*	19
Commuting with Nature	*by Nan Chalat-Noaker*	22
How Poison Creek Got Its Name	*by David Hampshire*	25
The Long, Open Spaces	*by Andy Cier*	33
The Making of a Mountain Dog	*by Amy Roberts*	35
Sage and Time	*by Jane Gendron*	38
Meandering	*by Teri Orr*	41
The Living Heart of Hope	*by Stephen Trimble*	44
My Park City Empire	*by Larry Warren*	53
The Man and the Land	*by Liza Simpson*	56
A Traveler Passes Through	*by Lisa Cilva Ward*	58
Original Thought in Round Valley	*by Lynn Ware Peek*	61
Growing Up PC	*by Caleb Case*	64
Empire Pass: Old and New	*by Vanessa R. Conabee*	66

Table of Contents: *Artwork*

Nest	*by Letitia Lussier*	4
Along Rossman Trail	*by Linda McCausland*	9
Park City Landscape	*by Alisa Livingston*	10-11
Sentinels	*by Mark Maziarz*	12
Park City's Great Barn	*by Felix Saez*	21
Eternal Motion	*by John Helton*	29
Silent Witness	*by Jan Perkins*	30
Orange, White and Gold with Allen's Hummingbird	*by Greg Ragland*	31
Moose in Aspens	*by Felix Saez*	32
Spiro Trail	*by Rick Pieros*	49
Round Valley	*by Gincy Carrington*	50
Three Little Birds	*by Renee Mox Hall*	51
Park City Winter	*by Dori Pratt*	52
Moose in Winter	*by Michael O'Malley*	55
Bluebirds	*by Letitia Lussier*	68
King Con at Sunrise	*by Sue Galusha*	69
Autumn Color	*by Robin Cornwell*	70-71
A Walk in the Lavender	*by Allison Willingham*	72

Front Cover Artwork: Open Space *by Stefania Barr*
Back Cover Artwork: McLeod Creek *by Linda McCausland*
Cover Design: *Liz Craig Myers*

Foreword
by Jane Gendron

Until the late 1990s, few Park City residents and visitors spent much time debating open space. Open space simply existed, seemingly in vast quantities. It filled the corridor from Kimball Junction, into Old Town; and, except where mining had deeply scarred the landscape, aspen groves, thick spruce forests and meadows of indigenous grasses and flowers (or chest-deep snow) covered the unbroken curvature of the alpine topography as it climbed all the way to Guardsman Pass, up Daly Canyon and spread across large swaths of land between subdivisions.

But then a new wave of "progress" arrived in all its glory. As the procession of excavators and scaffolding marched across the county map, folks began to realize that land owners (and who could blame them really?) were cashing in on development rights. It was time to speak on behalf of the land.

In 1998, a small group of artists and writers chose a gentle path to conservation. Under the guidance of a bookstore owner, the late Gary Weiss, and editor Cheryl Fox, these locals came together to bear witness to the crucial role open space played—and still plays—in Summit County. The book that grew out of this collaboration, the original *Park City Witness*, gave voice to the local land conservation movement. It also raised funds for the grassroots organization known as Conserving Our Open Lands, which became the Summit Land Conservancy in 2002.

As it turned out, plenty of landowners wanted a way to preserve their agricultural heritage. And plenty of locals and vacationers sought means to protect beloved places for recreation, wildlife habitat, clean waterways and world-famous Rocky Mountain vistas. After all, skiing with views of strip malls would put a nasty damper on the local economy; barbed wire barriers to hiking and biking trails would certainly spark revolution; fresh water downstream was just plain ol' vital; and, of course, we couldn't throw the wildlife out with the broken survey stakes.

Over the past decade, Summit Land Conservancy has facilitated more than 2,400 acres of conservation easements, including Round Valley, Empire Canyon, Fawcett Ranch, Judd Ranch, McPolin Farm, Osguthorpe Round Valley Ranch, Miss Billie's and Quarry Mountain. And hundreds of additional acres are edging from the limbo of negotiations to the promise of protection for perpetuity.

This second edition of *Park City Witness* is intended to serve as a celebration of open space, a reminder of the selfless acts of landowners and the ongoing need to save land. It is a collection of original essays and artwork, testimony to the power and beauty of these sacred—in the broadest theological sense—places. Lives, livelihoods and land intersect in these pages. And the common theme that runs through each and every story: gratitude.

Open space is not a mirage because this community makes it real. And so, we thank you.

J.G.

Park City Area 1998

Photo: *U.S. Geological Survey*

"One way to open your eyes is to ask yourself, 'What if I had never seen this before? What if I knew I would never see it again?'"
Rachel Carson (1907–1964)

Park City Area 2012

Photo: *USDA Farm Service Agency*

"Everybody needs beauty as well as bread, places to play in and pray in, where nature may heal and give strength to body and soul alike."
John Muir (1838–1914)

Introduction: Demonology
by Cheryl Fox

The basis for optimism is sheer terror. —Oscar Wilde

Devil's Tower. Devil's Slide. Devil's Postpile and the Dirty Devil River. The pioneers who ventured out West from the comfortable, tree-sheltered streets of the East evidently found Satan all across God's Country. Faced with the grim challenge of scratching a living from among these high desert valleys and surrounded by a horizon of granite teeth gnashing a biting sky, it is no wonder they saw their struggles mirrored in a landscape scarred by demons.

Today, we have mastered the inferno. Insulated from the reality of winter and the vagaries of the harvest by the controlled heat of internal combustion, we are now much more likely to see the gossamer of angel wings in the cloud draping its veil over the mountain's shoulder.

Of course the natural world is all of this and none of it. And that is why we need it, need it like we need water or love or God.

We need the leaf-strewn trails where we can listen to the crunch of our passing footsteps and all that signifies. We need the path that brings us to face the improbable moose and wonder at the epic evolutionary battles that created such a creature. We need the space to feel the implacability of rock and wind as our body gasps for steady breath.

The natural world challenges our physical reality and nurtures our essence, inspires our vision with perspective. Out here, we find the incomprehensible, the void, truth.

Open space represents everything that civilization is not and that it fears. Today we might be laughed at for seeing the hand of evil in the landscape, but people still seek to trivialize or tame or dismiss the power found in a grove of trees or in the holy light of alpenglow. Civilization insists that we pave the earth with explanations or buildings or anything concrete enough to drive away the devils that lurk in our own imaginations.

This is why we must save those open spaces.

More and more studies show that our need for nature is real. Children who grow up with the opportunity to play in nature without adult intervention develop an environmental ethic; time spent in nature enhances our memory and reduces stress (unless, perhaps, our nature hosts mountain lions). Someday when we fancy we've explained the human soul, I'm sure we'll find that it too benefits from the unfettered view of wild geese flying beside the mountain, or the arresting beauty of a wildflower blooming unexpectedly.

Poets, painters, philosophers, those whose introspection enriches our lives need nature too. The natural world grants us reprieve, insight, health, clarity, focus for our inspiration, and space to fill with art.

As our technology draws us together in teeming cities, we forget and ignore our fundamental connection to the earth and the wind and the living things that don't need us. This is a tragic, and possibly, fatal loss because it blinds us to the disastrous impacts we are having on our planet.

So let's not lose it. Surely people who have the power to conquer winter and distance and make light as if by magic can recognize the fundamental importance of the ground below, behind, and before us.

Ultimately, the natural world doesn't need us. The earth will reclaim the shopping center at Kimball Junction just as it reclaimed the cities of the Pharaohs or the temples of the Mayans. But we don't really have that kind of time.

Fourteen years ago, I wrote the introduction for the first *Park City Witness* and told of meeting a baby backhoe on my favorite trail.

That incubus was the harbinger of the sky scraper that blotted out that trail, and the clematis, and the elk who shared it with me.

Is evil just a matter of perspective? Today we face unprecedented challenges to our natural environment. Solving this problem is the moral challenge of our century. The question we must ask is not "what can I do?" but "what is the right thing to do?"

I encourage you to read this book. Then go out to the trails, the mountains, the creek that you have helped to save. Watch for angels or demons and the messages they send, and then bear witness...

Cheryl came to Park City to teach skiing to four year-olds in the fall of 1987. Twenty-five years later, she still teaches skiing, weaving this job in and around her work as Executive Director of the Summit Land Conservancy and her hobby of writing novels. She and her husband have two daughters who love to ski and sail and make up stories.

Nest
Letitia Lussier

I LOVE THIS PLACE. THIS PLACE DOES NOT LOVE ME BACK.
by Joe Totten

I am allergic to just about every exotic, native flora this land produces. Cheatgrass, Blue Gama, Indian Grass, you name it and I'm allergic to it. And it's not just the grasses. I react with watering eyes and headaches to most of the native and non-native trees in Summit County. Oak, elm, mesquite, pine, sage. If the tree or shrub produces pollen, chances are I'm allergic to it.

I'm not complaining. Regardless of my health issues, I wouldn't live anywhere else. My allergies are a constant reminder of the powerful force this land exerts on me. The land's beauty is grounded in its inflexibility. This terrain will change you, you will not change it.

Utah is an extreme landscape inhabited by extreme people. The summers are hot and dry. The winters are cold and snowy and seem to go on forever. The wind blows constantly. The soil is hard and rocky, less than 3% of the state is suitable for crops.

My first summer in Park City, I took my daughters for a walk in Round Valley. The sun was shining as we started up the trail. Within a few minutes the rain came and then hail. On our way back, the hail turned to snow. As we reached our house, the sun came out again. Four seasons in the space of a few hours.

It's little wonder the severity of this land has always attracted extreme personalities. The first non-indigenous inhabitants were religious refugees chased from the Midwest. They walked across a thousand miles of desert pulling everything they owned in over-sized wheelbarrows. Promised a green, lush Eden to establish their spiritual kingdom, they found Utah.

They planted crops, dammed the rivers and subdued the Native Americans. And slowly, over many years, a strange transformation took place. The extreme contrasts of terrain and weather left a permanent mark on their psyche. Years of drought, locusts, heat, wind and acute isolation helped produce some of the most stubborn, inflexible citizens in the country. At the same time, the harsh landscape forged the most self-reliant, kind and welcoming people I have ever met.

Isolated from the rest of the world, the pioneers took on the characteristics of their new home. They inhabited the land and over time the land inhabited them.

The land continues to make demands of those who have been here for generations or visitors who just arrived yesterday.

You can walk the southern deserts in the middle of July, a landscape as harsh and unwelcoming as the other side of the moon; and the next day stroll through a field of flowers in Christmas Meadows under a sky so blue you'll question your vision.

This extraordinary terrain demands you change to fit into the landscape. If you want to live in Utah, you are required to make a tangible sacrifice: your comfort, your health, your salary. You must earn your residency. If that sacrifice makes you a little odd at times, if you get a little defensive explaining why you have chosen to raise your family in Utah, well, that's the price of admission.

I don't have to fight drought and locusts to survive here, but I still have to deal with the isolation and the voracious developers. The snowplow comes by early in the morning so I can drive the 25 miles to the city, a trip that a hundred years ago took a man on horseback two days. I have it a lot easier today and yet the same forces are at work now as there were 150 years ago.

The landscape continues to apply a powerful force on my personality. Every day the heat or cold or wind asks: why do you choose to live here? And every day I give the same answer.

To live in Utah is an overwhelming aesthetic phenomenon that often defies explanation. To appreciate its beauty you must experience the landscape at ground level. Walk the trails, climb the rocks, ride the single-track, ski the mountains. Once you've done that...

On second thought, forget everything I've said. I don't want any more people to move to Utah. We have enough here already. Stay where you are.

Joe Totten's day job is Creative Director for McCann-Erickson in Salt Lake. When the sun goes down, he writes fiction. Joe and his family have called Park City their home since 1996.

Nowhere Elks
by Chris Waddell

My warm cracks the early morning summer cold. It's good. It comes from within—from the work as I pedal against the incline, rising above the sleep bed that I've recently left. Pulling and pushing breath brings meditation, gaining rhythm and solitude, which is shattered in a moment by a primal musk and fear.

Could I have made myself prey? Could a mountain lion be stalking the switchbacks? The Kenyans wear masks on the back of their heads because a cat won't attack if you're looking at it. I think that's how it goes. I don't have a mask. Do I go up? Do I turn around? If a cat is here, it's already seen me. My rational mind attempts to strip the truth from my imagination. I pedal, waiting, and cursing myself for waiting.

Traversing toward town, light shatters at the horizon, ladling its touch in tiny pools. Each turn awakens another part of town with another touch of light. It slips into the folds of the surrounding mountains—folds I won't see later in the day. It caresses the steeple, even though I know it's not a real steeple, above Park City Mountain village. Warmth rides the rays soothing the sting of cold that I'd forgotten was still there.

At the top, in the light, the musky scent hangs like last night's nightmare, or maybe like one from many lifetimes ago.

Chris Waddell is the winningest mono skier in Paralympic history. He's a member of the US Ski and Snowboard Hall of Fame, the Paralympic Hall of Fame, and a 12-year Park City resident.

Along Rossman Trail
Linda McCausland

Park City Landscape
Alisa Livingston

Sentinels
Mark Maziarz

Grounding
by Kristen Gould Case

Fourteen years ago, I wrote an essay for *Park City Witness* about how walking in the fields and meadows of Swaner Nature Preserve helped me sort through things in my life. At the time, one of my best friend's parents had just died in a plane crash, and I wrote about walking with my toddler sons in the meadows and letting my thoughts of sorrow for my friend and gratitude for my own happy life blow through the blades of grass with the breeze. I wrote about how watching the sandhill cranes moving so gracefully made me dream of a day when I might be a more mature woman who was unhurried in her ways. And how the meadows were always there for me.

Recently, my world came crashing down around me for a while. Everything goes into slow motion when your doctor starts saying things like lump in your breast, diagnostic mammogram, needle biopsy, MRI, "rare cancerous tumor that if you don't remove can spread into your blood stream and kill you," lumpectomy, mastectomy, reconstructive surgery, drainage tubes, anesthesia and when could I schedule surgery?

There was so much to absorb, so many decisions to make. I turned to the open spaces that sustain me. I'd walk down to the little pavilion overlooking Swaner with my cell phone when I had to take calls from the doctor's office. Somehow, trying to sort out all of the medical jargon of tests and results and surgeons and appointments and thinking about the scary things going on inside my body seemed easier to handle when all that lay before me were expansive outside things – open meadows and hawks and blue sky and the mountains all around me in a circle like the supportive arms of a hug.

The only thing that kept fear from catching up with me or being paralyzed by anxiety was to be outside and to keep moving.

I took to the trails to think. *What caused this tumor? Thank god it's me and not my kids.* I walked on the paths of Willow Creek. Up in Round Valley. Around Flying Dog. *I had to have a mastectomy? Was the surgeon exaggerating the severity of this thing? And what did she say about reconstructive options?* I walked along McLeod Creek, the Rail Trail, Iron Mountain. And these were the stupid cosmetic questions, really. Who cared whether I had silicon or saline, whether I even bothered to build a new breast or not, or if I should just "go for the double D's!" as my friends jokingly suggested just to make me laugh.

It was the deeper questions, of course, that terrified me. *What if I die? What will my sons do without me?* Who else is going to tell them every day how much they are loved? I haven't taught them enough yet. They need to know to look again — every time, before they change lanes or pull through a stop sign; to not put their wool ski sweaters in the dryer; how to survive a night in the wilderness or out in a big city; how to navigate traffic jams, college frat parties, constellations, girlfriends, arguments with people they love. How to pack their suitcases and make spaghetti carbonara. How to stand up for what they believe in. How to soothe a crying baby, perhaps someday one of their own. How to take care of their health. And their hearts.

Walking every day was the only thing that kept me sane. I moved to the beat of this mantra in my head, "It's not going to kill me, it's not going to kill me." The doctor told me so. She said if I had the mastectomy, I should be okay. She said it. *It's not going to kill me.* I believe her. Feeling my sneakered feet hitting the ground, steady and measured, the soft turf accepting the weight of my worries with every step, the open skies accepting my hopes and prayers, I kept walking.

And then I ran. I ran because I am the luckiest woman in the world. Last summer, celebration of good health and the addition of one fake boob to the family culminated in running a ladies-only half marathon, here in Park City, with proceeds benefiting breast cancer research. Eight hundred lucky women showed up for that run, all wearing pink. It was quite a sight to behold, especially since it snowed that morning. The tribe of lady runners along our trails in the snow looked like pink polka dots on a white sash that ribboned through 13 miles of our neighborhoods and our open spaces.

We ran on the gravel of the Rail Trail, by the little park in Prospector, the cattails of the North 40 fields, McLeod Creek's willows, past the White Barn and its historic ranchlands and by the Scarecrow Festival display along the bike path where, a week earlier, I had helped to decorate a scarecrow with a pink boa in honor of breast cancer awareness month. We ran the Willow Creek trails, looping around the meadows and the craggy cottonwoods, over wooden bridges and past the Wallin Barn. We ran under arches of aspen trees and past meandering creeks and buck fences and long grasses and the mountains, their orange and red autumn plumage dusted with snow. We ran past the shock and the fear and the anxiety and the worry. We ran to the newfound and profound perspectives on our lives. We ran to our healthy, unhurried futures, and we ran into the arms of our girlfriends, husbands and children. The finish line overlooked the meadows of Swaner Nature Preserve. I had come full circle.

Park City's open spaces center me and nourish me. They ground me and they lift me up. I press my feet into the earth of our trails and I feel my strength. I take long, deep breaths of the landscapes around me, and I know that I am okay.

Writer Kristen Gould Case is a 25-year resident of Park City. She is the editor of Park City Magazine, *and has published numerous articles in national magazines. She enjoys Park City with her husband Mark and her sons Caleb and Jesse.*

Galligan's Bowl
by Karri Dell Hays

Behind my house there is a parking lot and every morning, every day of the week for 365 days of the year between the hours of 8 and 9 a.m., this parking lot fills with the cars of parishioners going to Mass at Saint Mary's Catholic Church. But the rest of the day, the lot is empty. On any given afternoon, the neighborhood residents come to use this large paved area for various activities: throwing balls, walking dogs, riding bikes. My boys practice lacrosse, toss footballs and play hacky-sack. Occasionally, I join in too. Like the big backyard that none of us have, it has become a haven in our tight, hilly and painfully cozy, mountain urban neighborhood.

My situation is unique. I still live in the home where I grew up and I have raised my children with nearly the same lifestyle I had. The one thing that is vastly different between their world and mine is the fact that the parking lot behind our house was not a parking lot when I was a child; it was an empty, weed-ridden open area strangely called Galligan's Bowl.

It was in Galligan's Bowl that I played baseball, rode dirt bikes and discovered the boundless joys of snow.

Snow.

I still remember the first time I saw snow. I was three years old and we lived in Louisiana, of all places. On such rare occurrences, my mother bundled me up in a thin, powder blue parka with a hood that made me look like a little Easter elf. She stood me up in the sloshy, white mess in the backyard and giggled while she took a picture of me. Written on the photo is the word that I exclaimed as I gazed in wonder: "Milk!"

Only a few years later, my father discovered the sport of skiing and moved our family to Park City, Utah. As far as my three brothers and I were concerned, moving to Park City was the equivalent of landing in Santa Claus' North Pole — the one with ten-foot candy canes and flying reindeer. As we settled in to discover our new lives in the mountains, we quickly forgot the white sandy beaches of the south, the never-ending warm weather and the need for a swimsuit on a daily basis.

Each and every moment thereafter was filled with non-stop anticipation for the snow that would fall outside our 120 year-old miner's home. Once it finally started to fall, it fell often. I can still summon the itch and wriggle and fidget as we tried to sit in our dining room chairs. We listened without much regard to my mother scolding us to finish our dinners. Then, we bundled up in our still-wet clothes from the previous day's excursions and headed out to our snowy, polar paradise. There were snow forts to construct, jumps to build and tracks to run our plastic saucers and Hi-Flyer sleds. We gladly shoveled the steps and walkways of every neighbor before running — yes, always running — to dig tunnels and snow caves. They were the most difficult and we needed a lot of them in order to escape the overhead onslaught of the neighbor boys who pounced upon us with snowballs on a regular basis. Only our mother's definitive calls to "get your butts home right now" could stop our endless flow of excitement.

Then, there was the skiing. Every weekend and every other moment we could devise, we were on the slopes exploring every gully, knoll and chute. On whatever hill we found suitable, we built jumps so that we could practice our daffys, spread eagles, 360s and if we dared, a flip.

Today, my perspective of snow and this parking lot is a little different. I don't yearn to dig tunnels, build forts, do flips or take snowballs in the back of the head. But there are some things that still hold their power over me. When I stop, while skiing on a powder day, in a stand of frozen aspen trees and listen quietly to the sounds of their swaying and creaking, stiff in their sappy juices I am in complete awe. And when the trees hang heavy with sheaths of ice, dripping as if they were dipped in a sugary fondue, I can't help but giggle. As a child, I used to imagine that the sparkle of the bright sun on the glittery snow was an endless, elegant ball and the shimmer came from a sea of beautiful women and men who wore fancy, sequined dresses and suits, all spinning in a dance to celebrate the arrival of my favorite earthly element. On late night walks, I am entranced by the glisten of the moon on the white blanketed hills surrounding my town and I am reminded of my sweet, enchanted childhood.

As I walk across the now black surface of the parking lot that used to be my playground—and in some regards, still is—I pause to take in the fact that I still live in a fairytale world. To the east and down the slope leading to the back of my house, the frosted tips of my Russian sage and yellow rose bushes pierce through the heavy drifts, reaching for the sky, swaying in the shadows and hues of blue and gray—and milk.

Karri Dell Hays is a 41-year resident of Park City. She is a freelance writer and makes the best damn gumbo in town.

Mending Fences
by Tom Clyde

There are a lot of ways to interact with open space. Too much of the time, it is through the windshield of a car. In Summit County, we are more likely to be out there touching it—skiing, hiking, mountain biking, fishing, you name it. If it can be done outside, we will find a way to do it. We remember great hikes or bike rides. Encounters with wildlife stick with us, and we all have favorite trails or fishing spots.

A fortunate few of us get to experience open space on an agricultural level. What you call open space, I call business. Most of you drive past a farm field and enjoy the view. I drive past it and wonder why his alfalfa is taller than mine. Farmers know their land on an entirely different level. The connections are generational.

I saved a rotten cedar fence post that I replaced a couple of years ago. Above the ground, the post looks good as new. Below the ground, the post was rotted off to just the heartwood, maybe an inch in diameter. There are axe marks on it, where it was cut to length and where the branches were cleaned off the cedar trunk. It was probably cut when they cleared the land that is now the hay field. It's maybe more than a hundred years old. I have no idea who first built the fence, all those years ago. But I'm sure we employed a similar vocabulary when digging the hole in this rocky ground. We got 100 years out of it—good job, whoever you were.

As I work around the miles of fence on the ranch, different techniques of stretching and bracing barbed wire fencing show up. The same guy built a fence on the hay field and then a mile away around a pasture. The names are gone, but they left signatures in the way they twisted the wire, pulled the brace posts, and spliced the broken places. There are a couple of paths where the elk walk through the fence every winter, and the row of splices, and splices to splices, is a rich lesson in technique as well as farmer thrift. Better to splice the splice than pull a new wire that the elk will break again next winter.

There are signatures in the land, too. There are places where it takes two burly guys to drive a steel post into the rocks, and other places where the soil won't support them and the fence posts gradually sink under their own weight. The soil is different, even from one end of the field to the other. There are fields that soak up the irrigation water so fast that it is hard to spread it over the whole field. Fifty yards away, the clay swells, and the water runs off before it gets a chance to sink in.

You see things that are hard to explain when working the farm. I can go years without seeing a seagull at my ranch. But within a couple of hours of starting to plow up ground for a crop rotation, something that doesn't happen more than every three or four years, there are seagulls following behind the tractor. They feast on bugs turned up with the soil. How do they find out that there is fresh plowing 30 miles outside of their normal range?

The farm is constantly changing. Different trees cover the surrounding mountains at different times. Once they were pine covered. The bark beetles have killed off the lodgepoles, and the mountain is now more aspen than pine. The aspens are providing shade that helps start a new generation of fir. Forty years from now, the aspen-covered mountain will be a forest of firs. Nature rotates its crops, too.

Landmarks come and go. An aspen tree with huge bear claw marks in the bark has finally died and fallen down, though I remember trying to match my fingers to the claw marks so long ago that my father had to lift me up to see them.

You can experience open land on the drive-by plan, but you never really know it until you work the land. I'm just shy of 60 years here, and make surprising new discoveries almost every day.

Tom Clyde is a native Utahn and 30-year resident of Summit County. After practicing law for many years, he retired to managing his family's ranch in Woodland.

Park City's Great Barn
Felix Saez

Commuting with Nature

by Nan Chalat-Noaker

Usually, when there is talk about preserving open space, images of grand vistas come to mind—of spectacular slot canyons, untrammeled mountain peaks and raging rivers. But for most of us, our frequent encounters with nature take place on modest patches of accidentally undisturbed woods and pastures, along unnamed creeks and not-yet-subdivided foothills.

As a kid growing up in Detroit, I remember exploring a mysterious place of tall grass, squirrels and birds that was crisscrossed by footpaths worn in by kids in Keds and Schwinn bike tires. In retrospect, it must have been no bigger than a vacant lot amid a neighborhood of closely packed houses.

Later, I went off to summer camp, eagerly looking forward to swimming and canoeing among the thousands of anonymous ponds of northern Michigan and Wisconsin. Each year, my fellow campers and I wandered a little farther afield, broadening our perspective of the landscape and of ourselves.

The hook was set.

When I set out on my own after high school, heading back East and then out West, I always found a getaway somewhere on the edge of town that offered a little solitude and a chance to reconnect with nature—a wooded meadow or a deserted beach. Most of these havens were unofficial public areas on private grounds, used with the tacit but temporary consent of the landowners.

These days, the open space that satisfies that craving is served up on Brown's Pass, the nondescript rolling hills that form the no-man's zone that separates the cowboys from the skiers in Summit County. Like many local residents, I live on the East side and work on the West side, traversing Brown's Canyon twice a day in snowstorms and heat waves, year round, in early morning sunlight and on moonlit nights.

While the sagebrush- and scrub oak-covered terrain is basically unremarkable, the weather has a way of painting the scene in a new light each season. I have watched the snow pile up and melt away for 34 years, dodged deer and elk licking salt off the pavement in the dead of winter and laughed with relief at the first ground squirrel of the spring sprinting across the road. I've also seen owls swoop over the hood of my car and looked into the menacing eyes of a golden eagle sitting on a road-kill carcass.

The eight-mile, winding stretch of two-lane road gives me a chance to shift mentally from home to work. It's my time to sort through the day's priorities and, on the way home, to compose grocery lists, plan a dinner menu or fantasize about the upcoming weekend.

Often, though, amid the quiet, people-free landscape, the chaotic jumble of mental to-do lists and worries settles into the background. I inhale the fresh air, note a glint of sun off a rivulet of melting snow, or marvel at a massive cloud formation resting on Lewis Peak.

Sadly, the risk of falling in love with land that doesn't belong to you is that, someday, the rightful owner will decide it's time to build a subdivision or a shopping mall right in the middle of your little Utopia.

Despite its Wild-West veneer, the land both north and south of Brown's Pass is privately owned. Much to my chagrin, a good portion of it is zoned "Light Industrial." In between the hills and streambeds are several rock quarries, a snowmobiling outfitter, a smattering of houses, a water company and an animal-rescue ranch.

Over the years, the road has been significantly widened, new driveways have been carved into the hillsides and optimistic real estate signs have alternately sprouted and disappeared along the shoulder, each one jarring my daydreams and causing a moment of panic.

Friends across the county relate similar experiences. From the foothills of the Uinta Mountains east of Kamas to the upper reaches of Old Town in Park City, reports roll in of a favorite trail suddenly blocked by a locked gate or a menacing string of barbed wire adorned with No Trespassing signs.

Of course, that is exactly why we support groups like the Summit Land Conservancy, and what has motivated us, over and over again, to raise our own taxes to purchase and protect those disappearing bits of paradise.

Brown's Pass may someday be home to neighborhoods and schools, maybe even a Costco or an office complex. But, when that happens, I hope there will also be a section reserved for deer, elk and sandhill cranes, and footpaths for kids in sneakers and me. ●

Nan Chalat Noaker has been writing for The Park Record *since 1977 and she has served as its editor since 1996. During that time, she has watched the community struggle to balance essential economic development with careful preservation of its rural mountain landscape.*

How Poison Creek Got Its Name
by David Hampshire

I don't know how long the fish had been dead when I first spotted it. But it must have lain there for two or three weeks after that, on a sandbar where Poison Creek spills out of the culvert at the top of the Historic Union Pacific Rail Trail. Then, it was gone, probably washed downstream by one of those mysterious out-of-the-blue surges of water that periodically scour the creek.

I'm sure the fish was loaded with the heavy metals that have helped give the creek its name. But the fact that it had reached that point at all gave me a hint of the "purling brook" that had stirred the senses of early Park City resident Charles Street in 1874.

The brook was christened Silver Creek by Mormon explorer Parley P. Pratt in 1848, twenty years before prospectors found outcroppings of silver ore in the surrounding mountains. But it took only another 25 years of mining to turn the water so toxic that farmers downstream in Wanship had to stop using it for irrigation.

It was Rich Martinez who helped me put the pieces together, to understand how mining had served as a purveyor of poison and how the creek had spread that toxic brew over many acres of wetlands.

At the request of family members, I started interviewing Rich in January 2009 for an upcoming biography. Those interviews became my Thursday morning ritual lasting more than a year. Usually, I would park my car about 8:30 a.m. near the city bus garage on Short Line Road and walk up the Poison Creek Trail to the bottom of Main Street. En route, I'd walk past City Park, past a few kids rehearsing their moves at the skateboard park, past the make-your-own-music playground and the vacant lot once occupied by the Cattle Company Restaurant and boarding house where I moved in the summer of 1978. After that, I'd pass the Shoe Tree and then a pole with an empty metal box that once held an electric meter for one of the shacks on Easy Street.

Then, I'd take the sidewalk up the east side of Main Street, almost deserted at that time of day save for a few delivery trucks. If I hadn't dawdled too much at the Post Office, I'd be ringing the doorbell of his one-of-a-kind purple house on Daly Avenue right at 9 o'clock.

With the exception of a few months in the 1950s, Rich has lived all of his 77 years in Park City, most of it in Empire Canyon, which we now call Daly Avenue. He spent half a century working for the local mines and knows the underground workings about as well as anyone. Every Miners Day, he's the man with the microphone at the mucking and drilling contest at City Park.

Rich is a gentle man and a gifted storyteller. Our conversations wandered from his childhood memories to his years in the mines to his ownership of The Cozy, the iconic Main Street miners' bar. At my urging, he also talked about the milling process—how a half-dozen mills connected to the major mines would crush the ores and refine them into "concentrates" using mercury and other toxic chemicals. And the mills' waste products, the tailings? Why, they went right into "the ditch."

By that point, I'd been talking to Rich long enough to know that Silver Creek, Poison Creek and "the ditch" were one and the same. It just depended on how you looked at it, and when.

I did a Web search for "Silver Creek" in the old *Park Record* files and learned that so much mill waste had settled downstream that men known as "jiggers" were making a living by recovering and reprocessing the tailings.

Compounding the contamination were human and animal wastes. It wasn't uncommon to find outhouses perched right over the creek, a practice that continued into Rich's childhood. A 1906 letter in *The Park Record* warned readers that the creek was also being poisoned by "dead animals, cow barns and horse stables." In 1917, a state health officer's matter-of-fact report described Silver Creek as "the sewer system of Park City." What I found extraordinary in the officer's report is that he didn't seem to find this extraordinary at all.

Today, the creek flows obediently out of town in a channel just south of the Union Pacific Rail Trail. But it wasn't always there. It once formed a vast flood plain over the Prospector area, now covered with houses, condominiums, businesses and parking lots. And onto that ground, the creek deposited thousands of tons of tailings and other wastes.

By the time Rich was growing up in Park City in the 1940s, the creek had been moved, leaving mounds of dry tailings several feet deep as the perfect place for boys on their Schwinn bikes to create their version of a BMX track. *Contamination? What contamination?*

As a mine employee in the 1970s, Rich was part of a crew that hauled away most of the tailings, but enough remained in the soil to cause alarm among unsuspecting residents who, unaware of the area's history, had bought or built homes there. The city eventually worked out a plan that included covering much of the contaminated soil with a layer of topsoil. But other sites farther downstream are still being cleaned up. And removing the contamination from the bed of the stream itself appears to be a long way off.

Since my conversations with Rich, I've continued to walk the Poison Creek Trail. I look at that modest little stream and marvel at how it moved so much material so far.

Rich may have given me part of the answer. He told me the maze of mining tunnels has interrupted the flow of some underground streams that once fed the creek, diverting water into the Jordanelle Reservoir and the Spiro Tunnel.

I wonder whether the "purling brook" of Charles Street's time has much of a future. I'd like to think we're more enlightened than we were 95 years ago, when Silver Creek was literally Park City's sewer.

Now it's just the storm sewer. I guess that's progress.

David Hampshire is a veteran journalist who now works as The Park Record's *copy editor.*

Eternal Motion
2011, bronze, 80" h x 56" w x 48" d

John Helton Photo: *Dan Campbell*

Silent Witness, Marion Fields with Cows

Jan Perkins

Orange, White and Gold with Allen's Hummingbird

Greg Ragland

Moose in Aspens
Felix Saez

The Long, Open Spaces
by Andy Cier

Some *ethical vegans* don't eat honey because they believe that bees are enslaved in order to produce it. I am guilty of a similar crime: I coerce wild animals into building trails for me.

This confession is about my favorite piece of open space in the world. This particular piece of open space is two miles long but only two feet wide, and it meanders up the northern flank of a beautiful, wooded mountain covered in aspen and alpine fir, part of the farm where I live in western Summit County. Yes, it's a trail, and this one was created by myself along with the unintentional servitude of an elk herd, multiple deer, several moose, fox, coyotes, raccoons, chipmunks, squirrels and the occasional mountain lion.

That's why I feel just the slightest tinge of guilt for getting these various creatures to do my bidding. Building a trail all by yourself is a long, slow process. And I'll admit it: I'm lazy. But if, as they say, necessity is the mother of invention, then I point to my own laziness as the father. Buck mule deer, bull elk and bull moose are huge, somewhat lazy animals themselves; they just want to eat, sleep and procreate. I discovered that if you can help them accomplish these goals, they will do the work of a small army for you.

For several months of the year, male deer, elk and moose have enormous racks of antlers that weigh down their heads, get hooked on tree branches and generally get in the way. These big guys, unthreatened, will often take the path of least resistance—any safe trail that has room for their huge heads and isn't too steep. If you clear a path for their antler-laden craniums, their enormous bodies will follow, and with all that weight pressing down on relatively small hooves, their two pointed toes make the perfect tool for cutting a trail.

In plotting out this trail, I realized there were sections of game trails on the mountainside that already existed; segments of them ran at nice, gentle grades, but then would invariably angle steeply upward or downward. These natural deer and elk trails were perfect, little pre-made components of my eventual trail, but they were intermittent, randomly placed and often overgrown. I found, though, that if I took the brush I was clearing from my trail and used it to block the steeper sections of the game trails, the animals started using my trail instead, and started clearing it for me. Twenty or thirty elk running on the same path over soft earth make a mean trail. A bull and his harem will most often travel in a nice, single file line. If I made sure there was a clear path and plenty of headroom for the bull, then the whole group would use my intended path, cutting into the earth and creating a fine section of trail in five minutes that would otherwise have taken me 20 hours with a landscape axe.

During the project it turned out (much to my chagrin) that elk don't work for free. In creating this long, meandering trail complete with switchbacks and viewpoints, I had terminated it in our alfalfa field, where the elk did their eating, sleeping and procreating. Once I had them trained to work on the trail, I discovered the *quid pro quo*. Alfalfa. *We build your trail, you feed us alfalfa.* Over a series of years, our alfalfa field became a hay field, because grazing elk will chew alfalfa and hay down to the nub. Hay grows back. Alfalfa doesn't.

So what else did I learn from this decade-long experiment in wild animal domestication? To observe, to watch from a distance, to respect the quiet of the forest and strength of these huge animals. We all share a trail, and we inevitably cross paths. We have a quid pro quo with nature, and the "what" we take needs to be balanced with a "what" we give. And the best "what" we can give in Summit County is open space of any kind where wildlife can roam, perhaps guided to safety, but left, for the most part, undisturbed. ◖

Andy Cier and his wife, Lynn, have lived for the last 22 years in Park City, where they have raised three children. When he is not building a trail, Andy works in Salt Lake in marketing and advertising.

The Making of a Mountain Dog
by Amy Roberts

When I first moved to Park City in 2004, I was decidedly not a mountain girl. Back then, I thought of open space as an available parking spot at the mall on a busy Saturday.

But it's a funny thing when you move to the mountains—they have a way of moving you. Now, nearly a decade after declaring Park City my new home, I can't imagine my life without a "hiking happy hour" or a "backcountry breakfast."

Hiking, trail running, mountain biking, snowshoeing, camping, and backcountry skiing—they've all become part of who I am. I love getting lost in a maze of switchbacks with my dogs, Boston and Sabor, who fell in love with the mountains with me.

When we first moved to Park City, they'd never known anything but sidewalks, fences and the end of a leash. They were bona fide city dogs. Back then, they thought of open space as a crate-free living room.

Together, they happily became "mountain dogs" as I became a "mountain girl."

That pivotal transition in our lives started on the Spiro trail, a trail we've hiked as a pack countless times. There was something liberating, amusing and extraordinary about watching my two "city dogs" explore their new leash-less boundaries. Their curious expressions when they saw their first moose. The joy they seemed to find in freely chasing butterflies (and their tails). Their excitement over meeting other leash-free friends out for a hike.

Over the years, we've hiked, snowshoed, skied and biked hundreds, possibly thousands of miles together. And though many of them are simply routine wallpaper in my memory, there are some I will never forget.

When my grandpa died in 2009, Boston, Sabor and I climbed to the top of Iron Canyon, where I sat on the ridge and cried as they dutifully licked my tears. When my sister was diagnosed with brain cancer, we hiked Sweeney Switchbacks, where I rested under an umbrella of aspens and willed her strength and courage to fight, as my yellow mutt and Dalmatian somberly lay by my side. When I got a new job after being laid off, we snowshoed to the top of Lost Prospector. They ran ahead, breaking trail, seemingly energized by my joy and relief. When I later got promoted at that same job, we celebrated with a camping trip in the backcountry, where they were free to chase squirrels, take a swim in a snow-fed mountain lake, and then later dine on congratulatory gourmet milk bones under the stars.

These adventures all played a crucial role in my life. They are seared in my memory as poignant moments of growth, understanding, sorrow and delight. And they would not have been possible without protected open space.

Everything I love about Park City starts with open space. When you're a mountain girl (or guy, or dog), open space is nourishment for your soul. It enriches your life. It provides for quiet moments of reflection, inspiration, perspective and joy. It is, quite simply, what makes this town an exceptional place to call home.

Now, as my beloved 15½ year-old Sabor approaches the end of her life, her hiking days long over, I can't help but reflect on all the paw prints she's left on the trails that hug Park City. While losing my companion will surely be one of the most difficult and painful experiences of my life, I find peace in knowing the last half of her life she enjoyed as a mountain dog.

When that sad, sad day comes, as brokenhearted as I'll be, I will find comfort in the open space that surrounds me. It is there I will spread her ashes. So that her final resting place is the same place she began her new life — as a mountain dog.

Amy Roberts is a freelance writer and public relations executive. She spends her free time exploring the globe, but so far, her favorite spot is atop a snowcapped mountain overlooking Park City.

Sage and Time
by Jane Gendron

This trail is my morning cup of coffee, my evening glass of wine. I hike, run or snowshoe its switchbacks and let nagging thoughts and stress unravel in my wake. Some mornings, taking the lesser traveled loop requires waving my hands in front of me to clear silken threads, destroying the work of late-night creatures. Some afternoons, when the sun has weakened the snowpack, I fall through—post-holing my way to the relative stability of more shaded spots. I've sprained ankles, flipped over handlebars and bushwhacked my way around moose. I've stopped to look through the aspens at patches of cobalt sky and felt the heady freedom of a mountain bike descent.

I know every switchback. I remember the old path and I've adapted to the new.

I have photos, stacks of them. But I rarely brandish my camera, once I've ventured beyond the trailhead marker. The trails and the land form an unintended collection of memories, rivaling the most beloved photo album. A step into the cool shade of a particular stand of aspens or the scent of a wild rose can send me back a day—or 14 years. Just past where the trail kisses the ski run, I look for the startled red-tailed hawk swooping skyward with a snowshoe hare in her grasp, leaving scarlet drops on the fresh snow. Beside a crumbling mine relic, I pause to listen for the bugle of the roaming elk herd. Along a sun-drenched stretch of path, I smile at the two year-old version of my son, proudly proving his independence as he stumbled along, torn between keeping up with his dog and the joys of sunflower picking and pebble tossing.

For years, I explored our alpine meadows, groves and peaks, vaguely aware that I was passing through ski resort acreage, private property and open space. As rough-sawn timber, elegant ironwork and sheets of inviting-the-outside-in glass uprooted the wildflowers and aspens along certain paths, I came to understand that my trails weren't really mine after all. Even when the very place where my now-husband got down on bended knee was cordoned off with flexible orange plastic fences, I soldiered on with willful ignorance. I returned at twilight, when the bulldozers and excavators sat quietly; I skirted boulders until my pregnant belly seemed to rebuke my foolhardiness. As it turned out, our simple hike-to hilltop — we christened it Proposal Point — had billion-dollar views.

I've adapted. I've even acquiesced. I've taken the funicular, clinked cabernet glasses, eaten fondue and admired—yes, admired— the expansive terrace with its wall of fire, which sits directly in the path of Proposal Point. I've gone through the stages of grief regarding that particularly sacred place, the one where we drank cheap champagne and toasted our future with Mother Nature our only witness. And I suppose I understand that the land was never mine to lay claim to. But, I'm quite certain my maternal instinct would trigger fight rather than flight should the trail closest to my heart—the steep one with the switchbacks, aspens, woodpeckers and mine relics—suffer a similar fate. Part of it has been shielded from any future backhoe visits, but part of it has not.

As my little family has grown, my coffee-wine trail has become more of a Goldfish-warm milk stroll. Small children have a way of slowing you down as life seems to speed past at an unnerving rate. The mundane becomes the marvelous. In this world, magpies share the same rank as bald eagles and a flat rock, noted for its snack-worthy physique, outranks any summit. In my sons' eyes, I can keep this trail just as it is. Willful ignorance simply won't do.

I have a habit of picking a sprig of sage, rubbing it through my fingers and taking a deep breath almost every time I hit the trail. I don't know why I do it, except that the earthy, purifying smell forces me to pause and be grateful. It feels right to revel in my own insignificance here in this place of near-wilderness, where time is marked by sage-scented moments. Here I can retrace most of my dusty, muddy, snowy or leafy footprints. And layers of memories swirl and gather like a blizzard, an accumulation of lives, images, thoughts, fears and joys that are not just my moments, but collective experiences of a community. After all, no trail is mine. But some are ours.

My wish is simple. When I am an ancient, let me bring along my equally ancient dog and a thermos of tea and walk to this place or that place, bringing a gentle whisper of conversations to life. Let me point out the dancing aspen leaves to grandchildren, trace my finger along a frosted branch and follow the dainty prints of a deer. Let us count ourselves lucky that this land—which we belong to rather than the other way around—has been set aside for all of us to roam, laugh, think and cry. And let us toast the trail ahead. May it be there long after the sun sets.

Jane Southey Gendron writes for local and national publications. She and her husband Greg enjoy the happy chaos of raising two small boys and an overly friendly golden retriever in this tremendous mountain town.

Meandering
by Teri Orr

When I moved to town, it was called, Kids Creek. There was a little bridge, over rushing water, a few blocks from our new home. I was told old-timers gave it the name because it was an easy place for children to learn to fish. Grown men left the area alone. It was one of the few bodies of water in town that ran consistently. Having moved from Lake Tahoe and its surrounding river and creeks, I missed bodies of water most of all.

There was a dirt path along the edge of the creek and enough foliage you didn't notice you were a half a block away from a state highway. Lots of colorful birds were always in those bushes along the water, and their names were new to me. The grasses were flattened most mornings, at different times of the year, when the deer slept there. There were no houses in the immediate area, just open fields. Cow pastures. A bit of wildness.

Our house, which we rented for years before we bought it, was part of a new subdivision on the edge of town. After us and until you reached the junction, there was a farm here and a ranch there, but there was no other grouping of homes. It was all privately owned but to the eye, it was all open space.

We would walk there, my little family of a boy and a girl and me. Have a picnic. Throw sticks and leaves in the water and watch them move down stream. It was always very cold water and it rarely ran very high.

In some kind of crazy, time lapse photography of my mind, the clouds race against the sky from day to night and the children grow tall and there are homes everywhere. Filling in those cow pastures and wildness. The open space, where the ranches and farms used to be, all the way out to the junction. The hillsides, where there had been endless aspens, creating patchwork quilt colors in the fall. Homes suddenly everywhere.

The creek was renamed something far more proper, McLeod Creek, after the new subdivision of the same name. Homes backed up within a field or so from the water. There was a buffer, but barely.

My visits there became more frequent when my kids left for college. When the engagement was broken and my tears splashed and blended into the rushing water. I changed jobs after a long walk there, where the sun stayed on my face and the birdsongs lifted me and I followed my stick down the creek with the funny S turn, as I walked along the dirt path.

In my new line of work (a dozen years ago), I helped bring Tibetan monks to town; these gentle souls created a sand mandala for healing. In a show of impermanence, they traditionally sweep up their beautiful work at the week's end and pour the sand in rushing waters to bring blessings to the community. I knew just the spot to take them. And on a crisp fall morning, a handful of folks walked down the now-paved path, with the monks in their saffron-colored robes, and we all took turns returning bits of colored sand to water.

There is a bench in that spot now.

In the past few years I have rested there. I have taken a beverage and a notebook and written there. I have taken my sorrows and released them there.

The grasses are still flattened many mornings where kingfishers and mountain bluebirds and flickers and finches, still inhabit the fields and foliage. It is a much busier path most days. Runners and bikers and strollers and dogs and power walkers pass one another with purpose.

Meanderers are few.

The grandchildren have been to the creek, on foot and on bikes. We have taken picnics and rested on the bench and tossed sticks in the water and watched them float downstream. I have pointed out the names of birds in the bushes and explained why grasses are flattened. We have scooped up cold creek water to drink with our hands.

I haven't told them (or their parents) yet, when the time comes, I want my little bits of "dust to dust" to be tossed in there. Washed away. I have only recently come to this conclusion.

Sacred places aren't always cathedrals of glass and stone. Nor are they exclusively remote vast wilderness, where powerful forces of nature take your breath away.

Sometimes, they are within walking distance.

Teri Orr has been watching open space disappear around Park City for 33 years. She has written a column in The Park Record *for all of those years.*

The Living Heart of Hope
by Stephen Trimble

Stephen Trimble wrote this piece for the ceremonial groundbreaking of the Swaner EcoCenter in Park City, Utah, on October 3, 2006. Musician and storyteller Hal Cannon, Forrest Cuch of the Northern Ute Tribe, Summit County Commissioner Sally Elliott, Mayor Dana Williams, and Preserve co-founder Sumner Swaner also spoke.

GROUNDING

The Wasatch Mountains stand as a boundary between major continental truths. Mountain and desert. Urban and rural. Tamed and wild.

These mountains ground us. We stand here at the edge of these meadows in the Swaner Preserve and look up to high peaks, reassured. Today, in autumn, the near ridges are soft-textured, angles and shadows made from orange oak and red maple and golden aspen as if a linen handkerchief was lightly dropped, to crumple and cling to the tender earth.

Boundaries: when we begin to make sense of where we are, we start with boundaries. The political boundaries map out the overlapping hierarchies and jurisdictions and generations of ownership. Ecological boundaries separate wet meadow from riverbank forest from Gambel oak thicket from sagebrush-covered hillside.

Boundaries can help. And boundaries can hinder. They give us context, but they obscure connections. The connections remind us just how permeable the boundaries, how downright ludicrous our lines on a map. Start with the water flowing across the meadow in these small creeks. Do you know where those creeks are headed? The children who come here will know. They will learn about their home landscape. They will trace the water that gives us life in the desert.

Upstream lie the mountains—the ski areas, the high ridgelines. The Olympic racecourses. Jupiter Bowl, Daly Canyon. Snowmelt feeds the small streams that course across our meadow and into East Canyon Creek. Follow the creek, and you will run from the Preserve to Jeremy Ranch and down the old Mormon Trail and Pony Express routes to East Canyon Reservoir.

The rain that came yesterday will filter through the wetlands of the Preserve, into the creek, finding its way from East Canyon Reservoir, north to Morgan Valley, into the Weber River, through the rapids of Weber Canyon, on through the city of Ogden, the irrigated fields of the Weber Basin Project, and into the Great Salt Lake at Ogden Bay.

And so this water that nourishes meadows here will grow our food west of Ogden and replenish our magical inland sea and its billions of brine shrimp once it reaches the Great Salt Lake. We stand in the headwaters of a desert river.

Listen to the Preserve for just a moment.

We are listening for silence. We are straining to hear the liquid whistle of a red-winged blackbird, the high wild eerie call of a red-tail. At night, we would hope for coyotes.

But we heard not just the riffle of wind or the gurgle of Spring Creek. We heard the vacuuming of the red-backed leaf blowers, the hum and bustle at Redstone Center, the rumble of Interstate 80. The highway passes right through this Preserve, connecting it to the life of the nation, for if those trucks drive to the next stop sign, they will go west to San Francisco, east to New York City. And that's okay.

For this wild place isn't wilderness. Generations of people have washed over the meadow in waves. Development surrounds us. We can hear it. We can see it. And yet here we have this place that protects habitat and creatures, ecological diversity and integrity, right next to our homes. The Preserve reminds us that wildness flows through our lives. Always. Everywhere. This place will be the door to that world.

Here, we introduce our children to their home landscape. They will take these experiences along with them on their journeys. Our job is to create the possibility of connection—to be thoughtful matchmakers between our children and the Earth.

CONNECTIONS

Inevitability and chance bring the generations washing through these meadows. Forrest Cuch and his Ute people—and their ancestors. Wave after wave. Some combination of inevitability and chance brought Hal Cannon's family here, so he could sing for us and tell stories of helping with stock drives down Park City's Main Street as a teenager.

With a few twists of chance, I might have joined him on that cattle drive. My mother's family followed their relations to the western frontier to sell clothing to the miners. If their cousins had been in Utah instead of Montana, perhaps they would have moved to Park City instead of Butte in 1880.

My father came from a North Dakota farm family. The bust came in 1912, when my great-grandfather lost his money in the wheat futures market. Cleaning out his office, he found the forgotten deed to an apple orchard in Washington. It was all he had left. And so the Trimbles moved to the Yakima Valley, where my father grew up. But that orchard could have been in Heber Valley. The deed could have been to an alfalfa field in the Snyderville Basin. Chance is powerful.

Some other unique combination of chance and inevitability brought the Swaner family to this meadow. The clan gathered here in 1993 after the death of their father, deciding what to do with this land. They chose a tender act of restraint, acting in the face of what my writer friend Alison Deming calls "the disease of American heroic individualism."

The Swaner family took their stand against the tide of every-family-for-itself and began talking with their neighbors, gradually building a 1200-acre preserve from the original 190 acres. In this way they embraced the immediate community—and now they have invited all of us into this open space.

And so we build outward, from the Swaners themselves, to other owners who chose to build the Preserve, to the community concerned with its future. The Park City community endures all the pains of explosive growth, part-time residents, huge turnover in its citizens, raids on its remaining public land. This makes the choice we have taken here all the more precious, all the more remarkable. Miraculous. Visionary.

The opposite of relationship is arrogance. The arrogance afield in the world today brings enormous loss and grief to us all. The antidote is community, relationship, hope.

The paradox of preservation of these wetlands challenges us constantly to think about how we make our decisions about what lands to save. How do we arrive at our devil's bargains about open space. Which of our Edens do we choose to preserve?

Eighty percent of people in the West live within five miles of streams and wetlands or former streamside woodlands. And yet, or perhaps, because of this, 90% of riverbank woodland has been destroyed in the desert West for flood control and irrigation.

In the face of despair, we have taken a stand here at the Swaner Preserve. A stand against loss. A stand in favor of survival, a stand that looks to the future, a stand that places us within Wallace Stegner's "geography of hope." We have chosen long-term preservation over short-term ownership, collaboration over conquest, respect and love and trust over quick profit. The Swaner Preserve is common ground for community.

Why do you care about open space and marsh habitat and spotted frogs? I'll wager your path began in childhood. Playing in marshes and fields. Catching frogs (and letting them go, of course). Fishing in streams. Staring at clouds.

Memories like these lodge in our hearts and change the way we live. The children who come to this meadow will have experiences here that will stay with them throughout their lives. Their relationship with the earth will grow from these seeds, in class field trips, in summer visits poking around in the Preserve. Aldo Leopold wanted young people to grow up with a blank spot on the map of their childhood, and for the children of Summit County, this is it, for it's accessible to all.

Our children. New residents—trying to make sense of their adopted home ground. Travelers passing through, maybe just staying a night at the hotel next door—and looking for guidance into the soul of our home landscape.

For all of us, this Preserve is the living heart of our geography of hope.

As writer, editor, and photographer, Stephen Trimble has published 22 award-winning books during 35 years of work with Western landscapes and peoples. Trimble makes his home in Salt Lake City and in the redrock country of Torrey, Utah. His website is www.stephentrimble.net.

Spiro Trail
Rick Pieros

Round Valley
Gincy Carrington

Three Little Birds
Renee Mox Hall

Park City Winter
Dori Pratt

My Park City Empire
by Larry Warren

It would have been close to 40 years ago when I first discovered Empire Canyon. I don't remember exactly. I would have walked up Main Street and kept going, past the funky miners' shacks that lined Daly Avenue, past ramshackle Bea's Canyon Lodge and the falling down garage further up that still hasn't fallen to this day.

The hike went past a curious concrete building with "J.M. & S. Co. 1920" molded into the cement gable. Inside was a shamble of round rock drilling cores, once carefully stored on numbered racks but now scattered and broken by vandals. To the east was a small railroad track that entered an open, lean-to side of the building where I heard running water. The water was down in a deep dark hole. I threw in a rock, never heard it hit bottom and carefully stepped back. In a side canyon, another warehouse of the Judge Mining & Smelting Co. stood empty, except for more core samples. Nearby, I carefully explored an abandoned mine tunnel. It dead-ended after a hundred yards. Further up, a huge tailings pile covered part of the canyon. A small stream worked its way around the edge to continue downhill.

Beyond the tailings pile were other mine buildings and the head frame of the famous Daly West Mine. Twelve hundred feet below that head frame, 34 miners died a century ago, when the powder magazine exploded. And above all that mining detritus of a past century rose the heart of Empire Canyon. Here, my kids and I prowled, pretending we were prospectors. We'd find shiny, gold rocks. They thought they'd struck gold and we'd all be rich. It was iron pyrite—fool's gold, but still pretty and shiny.

Except for our Yellowstone trips, I'm sure the empty meadows of Empire were the first place my children saw moose in the wild. Every time we hiked or rode a bike there, we seemed to see them—

bulls with big racks pushing through the grasses. The high hillsides were pretty open with rocky cliffs defining the Daly Chutes, a future launching pad for double black diamond skiers.

Years went by and I started to notice survey stakes and headlines in the paper about development plans. I chalked it up to the inevitability of progress in a booming ski town. Aside from the drawbacks of construction on our hikes, positive things began to happen, too. Deer Valley Resort expanded lifts into Empire and built a day lodge worthy of a western national park. It became my favorite place to ski. Then, houses and condos no miner could have conceived in his wildest imagination began rising. And the tailings pile, filled with toxic heavy metals, was trucked away from its perch over Park City's watershed. The head of the EPA flew in to give the developer an award for cleaning up the mining mess.

Deer Valley began actively managing the forest. Much of it had been cut away by miners looking for shoring material inside the Daly West or saw logs for their shacks and mine buildings. The resort, working with the state forester, began inventorying the tree stands, thinning some to let in the sunlight and the powder skiers. The resort also spread native grass seeds, and still more moose showed up.

Knowing that much of Empire Canyon would become a future playground, the property's owners, the mining company, donated more than 1,080 acres of open space to Summit Land Conservancy to protect it for all time. The easement includes the marshes around Lady Morgan Springs. Moose and elk have bred there for more years than man has been around, including the bulls that seem to materialize whenever my kids and I arrive.

Mining devastated Empire Canyon. Men died underground. They were swept away by avalanches above ground because they'd cut the trees that held the snow. They buried the streambed with millions of tons of toxic overburden. There's a reason the creek running through old Park City was called "Poison Creek." You couldn't have found a more heavily impacted no man's land than parts of Empire Canyon.

I accept that it is now developed with the Montage Hotel, the Empire Lodge, the houses and condos of the Empire Pass development. They're nice looking, well-built buildings. People, including me, enjoy them. No one dies here anymore. No one has to worry about the water quality. Now, it's a place of recreation that brings joy to those who come here. The scars of the past are healing well and the land will be protected forever.

Some day, my children's children may come here. I bet they'll see a big bull moose.

Photo: *Michael O'Malley*

Larry Warren is a Park City-based broadcaster, author, columnist and documentary filmmaker. He has been a long-time advocate for public lands as a writer, lecturer and former Congressional aide in Washington, D.C. working on national parks, forests and western lands legislation. Warren is the General Manager of Park City's community radio station, KPCW-FM.

The Man and the Land
by Liza Simpson

The man, the woman and I meet in the plaza. The sun is warm with fall just beginning to add a hint of chill to the air. All around us, the aspen and Gambel oak are a riot of color, our reward for the wet and grey spring we had this year. We begin our hike at the trailhead near the plaza. We have a specific destination in mind. The man is moving slowly, due in part to his age, in part to his desire to stop and share. As we walk, we talk and laugh about our lives, our families, ourselves. He and I share a doctor and we laugh about how good and tough she is. She has gentle tolerance for her patients who don't follow her advice, but she sighs. We laugh about the weight of these sighs and all that they do and don't say.

We are here for a small celebration of sorts. The larger celebration has happened, a large party on the plaza with media and dignitaries, trail users and trail builders. The man's family was honored and feted for their decision to sell their land not for development, but for conservation. This property has many gifts that most will never see: a fresh water spring, aspens with trunks that my arms can't span, habitat for elk and porcupine, moose and hare, and more. And today these gifts are protected forever.

The trail exists to bring everyone into a piece of beauty; it is that trail we walk today. We climb, stopping to admire the water tower. The sun warms our backs.

Today is the culmination of years of conversations and long relationships connecting the family, the mayor, the woman who walks with us, the attorneys who helped frame the agreements, and those who will make sure this property stays the way it is today. When the man led some of us on a tour of the property before agreements were finalized, I promised him a picnic. That is why we hike today. As we get closer to our destination, the view over town expands. The picnic grows heavier on my shoulder. We have wine, cheese, bread, fruit, salad, and cool water.

All along the trail, we meet others: bikers, runners, dogs, all out enjoying the glory of the day. We introduce the man to everyone, explaining that the trail bears his family's name and why. To a person, they thank him.

Our destination is a favorite of the man's; now, it is enhanced with a stone bench. Looking out over town, we laugh as we contemplate an imaginary zip line, running across Park City to the PC Hill. The man talks about the change he has seen in the community over the many years his family has been here, and how good he feels about the path the community has taken. He talks about his latest projects on his adjacent property. He is a peripatetic builder, constantly improving the ranch below us.

We sit in the sun and share food, drink and stories. We start with a toast, and give thanks all around: to everyone who worked to make this happen and for the day. It is a meal meant for conversation, and meant for open air and panoramic views. Trail users stop and chat about how well the trail is designed, how beautiful the setting, how breathtaking the day. The conversation meanders for hours, through the meal, through the dessert and as we gather ourselves to head down the trail, we agree that this was a perfect day for enjoying this gift the family has shared with the community. We wander down the trail, stopping to take in the different vistas across town, and promise each other to do it again, maybe on snowshoes... 🌰

Liza has been on the trails, winter and summer, with two- and four-legged friends since 1989, supporting and celebrating our open spaces. Writing about our community and food—always food—is one of her passions.

A Traveler Passes Through
by Lisa Cilva Ward

I run the trail to sort out what I can control, and what I can't. Life is too hard sometimes, and the hardship goes on too long. From a starting point rooted in frustration that makes me brittle, I reach for running shoes and head for the trail as a necessary act of survival, a coping strategy: to exhaust my body and stretch my limits until the monkey chatter in my head stills.

Steps from my house, I'm on the Secret Trail, a less-traveled, unpaved route extending parallel to the Rail Trail. It's a private, narrow path, cooled by the shelter of overhead trees. Here and there are signs of where an animal slept for the night, a stone-circled indentation where someone has planted a sapling honoring a loved one, untrampled grasses standing hip-high. The trail soon enters a long, steep ravine, a deep cleavage of earth leading sharply up the mountain. I climb it with purpose, raising my heart rate quickly and marking a distinct separation between daily life below and a luxurious window of time when I am not available to others. To restore my reserves, I require solitude.

I am quickly out of breath, but I don't slow down. In seconds, an expansive view of town has opened behind me, and in front, nothing but aspen trees and scrub oak, tall field grass, wildflowers, buzzing bees, animal scat underfoot. The ravine opens at the top to join the Lost Prospector trail, and it's here that the weight I carry begins to fall away. A quick sip of water, strip off a layer, and I begin to run.

I sometimes spend the first half of my run cursing God. Wheels of complaint and resentment churn in ragged, grinding circles inside my head. I run with the rhythm of heavy steps, head hanging low, face squished with intensity. I spit and rant about burdens too heavy to carry, lack of fairness, self-pity. Once or twice I've scolded God for abandoning me and my loved ones.

But here's the thing about trail running: it's not the trail's job to make it easy for me. There is no pavement here. No, I've got to take the mountain on its own terms, accept the risks. While the trail might welcome me, it's my job to figure out how to maneuver it. The path itself is never smooth, and if I waste my attention elsewhere, say, entertaining monkey chatter about life's burdens, the moment between enjoying the journey and landing on my face is a fraction.

It's a technical process to run the trail, constantly scanning the surface a foot or two in front of my steps, to catch and manage obstacles. And that's what I like about it; I choose it because it's difficult. There are tree roots, fallen branches and low-hanging leaves, slippery patches of loose granular stones, sharp rocks, swollen pools of muddy clay, and sudden slopes that turn the surface in an unexpected direction. I must adjust with each step, hopping over a root here, vaulting off a boulder there, banking off a slope and then righting myself to maintain balance, all at running speed.

I run the trail daily from early spring to late fall, and the progression of seasons is reflected in which plants are still in bud, and which are in bloom. Today sego lilies open; tomorrow daisies; next week, rich purple asters and yellow columbine; then wild pink mountain roses and the scarlet petals of Indian paintbrush. In autumn, I run on a lush carpet of fallen aspen leaves. Twice one spring, a silver-white fox appeared at a specific curve of the trail, running just ahead before disappearing under brush. Catching my breath and thanking her for showing herself, I knew, too, that she wasn't granting me witness, but luring me away from her den. Because I am only a guest on the trail, a traveler passing through. With every step, the brush rustles as I pass, lizards diving under leaves, rabbits and chipmunks scurrying out of sight. Deer bound away from the sound of my footsteps, and on a rare occasion, I round a curve to find a moose that does not budge.

The trail and its inhabitants are generous, providing sanctuary to anyone who seeks it, available any time. Traveling through it, there is so much to absorb, one step after the next, that soon there is no room for mind chatter. I am the recipient of gifts, so lucky to be there.

By the time I arrive at the end of Lost Prospector, just before it drops down into the Skid Row trail, I feel as if I can run many more miles, indeed, keep going forever. I'm no longer out of breath and any anger or complaint I might have harbored has been spent. In its place I feel the simplicity of peace. There is a lovely, thick grove of aspen trees in that spot, with long slender branches that reach toward each other and join overhead. The trail runs right through the center of this shady shelter. It is private there, so quiet, so peaceful that I stop every time, close my eyes, breathe, and pray. I ask for strength, for patience. I ask for fortitude, that I might weather the challenges of my life and find growth in them. I try to return to a place of grace.

When I emerge from the grove and begin the long, glorious run down Skid Row to the Rail Trail, and the return home, I feel only joy in the nuances of generosity the trail has shared. My chapel is this ground, my pastor is in these obstacles, and the breeze that cools me is my verse. They demand much of me, and I am grateful.

Lisa Cilva Ward has been enjoying Summit County's beautiful open spaces since the autumn of 1981. Her favorite way to spend time is writing, as well as hiking and running our incredible trails.

Original Thought in Round Valley
by Lynn Ware Peek

They say there is no original thought. There must be, I muse, from my rock, the one from which I ponder life. The one at the top of the steep trail at the edge of the high meadow. I'm not one for trail names in Round Valley, so I can't really say where exactly. Round Valley is defined not by which trail you venture upon, but by the wonder you feel from being there. It's the place that holds the magic. The pockets of peace and tranquility, the corners of inspiration, the areas where I've told my secrets and the zones within Round Valley where I've struggled, rejoiced and where I have been exuberant, famished, parched. Where I've been both tapped of energy and have found my energy. Round Valley is a singular vortex that has held and protected all that is sacred to me for several decades now.

I remember a run through Round Valley with a young suitor two decades ago, the first time I ever ventured into the sage-filled, hidden valley—so close to the thriving town, but so far away too. He knew about it because he was from here. We crossed barbed wire fences with gentle protests from me, the rule follower. Should we be here? We turned ankles as we ran across the hillsides, nary a trail in sight. Since then, it's all a blur because each time I visit Round Valley, there's a new trail and a new place to go that holds something dear.

It's curious that there can be a geographical place that is as hallowed and revered as relationships with loved ones. I never thought I'd consider a space, with topography and geology, as holding the full experience of me – through all my incarnations and stages of life. But Round Valley is that place. As I sit on my rock and reflect on my non-original thought, I realize Round Valley is that place on Earth.

From my perch on that tabletop rock, I scour the ridgeline that encompasses Deer Valley, Park City, and Canyons. It's funny to identify mountains as the ski resorts they hold, but I do, because those ski resorts are as inherent to the make-up of Park City as the open space is. I picture skiing down that ridge over there, I check the ski conditions on the mountain in the winter, or scope out a new trail in the summer. I check the foliage that signals the passing of the seasons, and from that rock in Round Valley, I formulate my own weather report. Sometimes the anticipation of the weather is an exciting foreboding that can only be known from there, from the rock in the meadow on that trail whose name I can never remember.

I found that flat rock when someone told me that I should do breathing exercises and meditation. When I try to meditate during yoga class, I fall asleep. When they tell me to breathe, I can only identify with the breath I take in as I push my body up a steep incline or over rocks or around trees. It's being outside in nature, I realize, that gives me the meditation that speaks to my soul.

Being in Round Valley connects me to all that weaves experience into gratitude. I've loved Round Valley as a place of solace. And being there replays the tapes for me that encapsulate all the experiences that beautiful piece of open space gives: the moonlit night I skate skied alone with a headlamp and spotted the mountain lion and couldn't scramble back to the car fast enough; the time I escaped there after waiting in a three-hour Sundance Film Festival line and relished knowing that no one who got into that film got to see what I did in Round Valley. I marvel at my belief about my near death experience right there on the edge of a neighborhood. I was in a blizzard during a crazy ski race and had to talk myself through it as you might talk yourself down Everest.

I relish the stories I've been told by dear friends as we've frolicked through Round Valley; and the emotion I've spilled out from some lost love I've lamented. And I smile as I think of the secrets I've told to that rock — the one that's at the top of that steep trail, at the edge of that meadow. The rock from which I've gazed out at the most beautiful ridgeline as I'm experiencing the thought that seems quite original to me. ◗

Lynn Ware Peek is the creator and host of Tales from the Wasatch Back, *host of* The Mountain Life *and reporter at KPCW Community Radio in Park City. You can find her and her dog, Jack most days on Park City's open space. She lives in Park City with her two sons.*

Growing Up PC
by Caleb Case

When I was young, we lived a short walk away from a small meadow. In the summer, my mom would take my brother and me out in the baby jogger, down the street and then onto the dirt path that circled the meadow. Those are some of my earliest memories: bouncing down the path in our lime green twin baby jogger, looking at the tall yellow grasses that swayed in the breeze against the blue sky, smelling the baked heat that radiated from the dirt, listening to the steady squeak of the wheels and the tweets of the birds. It wasn't uncommon to see a herd of elk grazing there in the mornings, or to come across their droppings on the side of the path like little black mile markers. In the winter, we would take walks with the whole family, my brother a mop of curly hair sticking up from the bundle of clothes in my mom's baby backpack. The snow would shine brilliantly under the same blue skies, and the squeaky wheels would be replaced with that peculiar crunchy-squeaky sound that only new snow under your boots can make. The meadow and the rest of the open space in Park City was embedded in my childhood, not emphasized, but not ignored either, just there along with the colorful toys and gigantic relatives that filled up my life.

Things changed. The meadow was paved over and up sprouted a school in its place. Any kid's nightmare, right, playground turned school ground? The elk moved out, the tall yellow grass turned into painted yellow lines, the smell of hot dirt turned to sweaty children and burning asphalt and the sound of the birds chirping was overridden by rumbling buses and screaming school kids. It wasn't a heartbreaking moment, but it was sad, and the whole family was sad to see the meadow go, even if it did mean a brand new school within walking distance. But that was progress, and as my childhood progressed, so did the slow invasion. I started going for longer bike rides, and noticed that there was a new house or two every time I went out. We started taking our walks on the Rail Trail instead of our meadow, but there were enough houses and gas stations between home and our new stomping grounds that we had to pack into the car to do it. There was no grand, dramatic moment, but over time, the outdoors seemed to get smaller as I got bigger, and soon it felt like I lived in a town with pockets of country, instead of the other way around.

But the same way that meadow held me and taught me, the land around me today remains a constant part of my life. Whether I'm playing lacrosse under the watchful eyes of the mountains, skiing down mountains furred with pine trees or simply biking or walking through rolling hills of fragrant, dry sagebrush, the land is a part of who I am. If I look out my window while lying in bed, I can see the snowy peaks like a line of soldiers marching into the distance. Turn the other way, and I see rolling hills of snow and brush like a foamy ocean. The land has a presence all around, with strips of sage and grass stretching through the town like veins in a heart, all flowing with animals and people, circulating an organic, natural strain of feel-good energy throughout my town. Because it is my town—the town that raised me—that taught me what fresh crushed sage smells like, what new grass feels like between your toes, what fresh snow sounds like as it whispers under your skis, that showed me how important nature is, how utterly indispensable our connection to open air and stretching space is, and I never want that to change. For 18 years, the open land around me has played as much a role in raising me as the school systems or my parents have. It is a mentor that no child should miss.

Caleb Case has lived his entire life in Park City and graduated from Park City High School, Class of 2012.

Empire Pass: Old and New

by Vanessa R. Conabee

I came to these woods late. The looming precipice of Empire Bowl and forbidding trailhead had kept me from it, over the years, but once I entered I was gone—struck by a sense of largess, of the trail going in and deeper, instantly hooked by the rapid transition of *here* going to *there*. Here the meandering aspen gave way to thick pine forests charged with the scent of evergreen and metals; there became steep ravines flanked by lodgepole pines, steadfast and true. In a clearing, I met a moose that looked at me as if I were trespassing, and then the trail broke west and went straight into the hills, dipping and diving in roller-coaster fashion before gaining altitude and presenting the bowls of the next ski resort. After a long, flat, rolling traverse came an open meadow with expansive views of the surrounding valley before returning, once again, to the darkening wood. There is an intensity to the entire place, as if the narrow trail were an afterthought, a barely tolerated scribble far less important than the landscape encompassing it. I went in the morning and early evening; I rarely saw another person. The trail went on and on but it wasn't until I'd spent months running there that I finally reached the end.

There are elements of this place that seem other-worldly, or not meant to be seen: a place on a tree where the trails of interlocking beetles form a double helix, the tramped-down grasses of deer beds, a lone coyote trotting along the ridge. Sometimes, in the furthest recesses, there is a sense of being scrutinized by the rocks and trees and birds and branches, by the wind lifting up and sweeping back down to the earth. The light fades on distant hills and the day ends in gold borders; the stars coming out in the sky are astonishing. Every time is the same, but each time is like new; each time I return a slightly different person than when I left.

This gift of perspective remains one of the most important facets of open space: it puts me in my place. In a day and age where it has become the norm to share our private lives with a virtual audience it is even more critical to protect the places that grant us escape.

Solitude, in the words of Ansel Adams, *so vital to the human man, is almost nowhere.* It is good to get away, it is good to return to the places that remind us where we started, that give us the opportunity to remember and reflect. This place takes me away from routine and monotony, it is the stolen hour giving shape to my day. I may begin in a fog but before long the adrenaline kicks in and I am disappearing down the trail, body propelled over the earth. I am tireless, my head filled with the buzzing, humming, building anticipation of what comes next and I've abandoned myself to the hills, I am gone.

This is what I hope for when I pass through that trailhead, this is the response that fuels compositions in every medium. Now that I've spent enough time to recognize time itself is fleeting, this is what has become most important. To preserve what was lost, to bring back what was nearest, to replicate that which can seldom be bought and sometimes only faintly remembered. Give me what was, let me return, let me stay forever. I want that day never to end, the day I ran tirelessly and covered the hills, the day the air came easily and my feet barely met the earth. Although it passed in a blur I am still going through the paces, each rock and tree and branch and bit of sky flashing through the leaves sharp and singular for the living beauty.

Vanessa Reichartinger Conabee is a freelance writer and active mother of three.

Bluebirds
Letitia Lussier

King Con at Sunrise

Sue Galusha

Autumn Color
Robin Cornwell

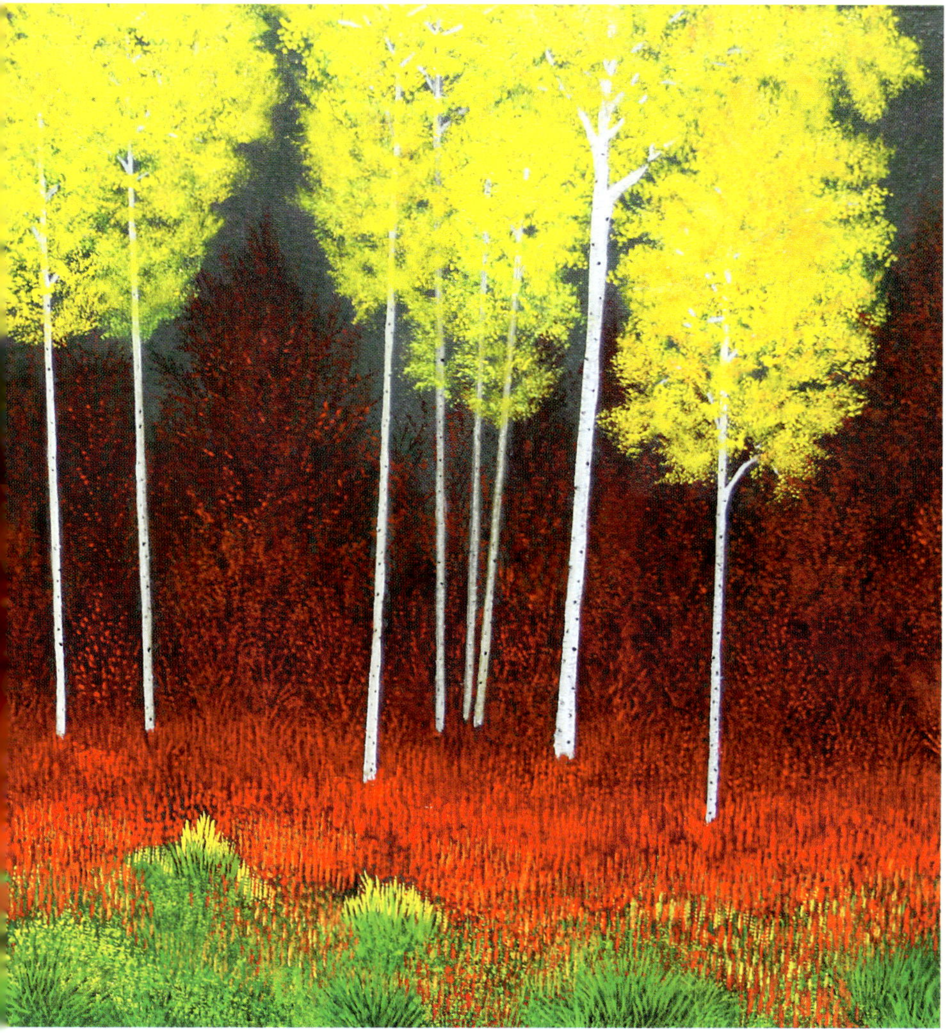

A Walk in the Lavender

Allison Willingham

WE SAVE LAND

The Summit Land Conservancy's mission is to work in partnership with landowners to permanently protect the remaining agricultural lands, view sheds, animal habitats, waterways, and rangelands in Park City and Summit County.

Awarded with accreditation by the Land Trust Accreditation Commission in 2011, the Summit Land Conservancy is one of only 158 accredited land trusts in the country, and the first in Utah.

The Conservancy holds 21 conservation easements on more than 2,400 acres of open space. Each time a new conservation easement is placed on a property, the Conservancy accepts a responsibility of stewardship that will last as long as the land itself.

The Summit Land Conservancy is a local advocate for open land, encouraging awareness, community dialogue, and creative win-win solutions for everyone in Summit County. For many years Summit County was one of the fastest growing counties in America. This growth provided opportunities and benefits, but many people feared that we would lose the open spaces that defined our community character. The Summit Land Conservancy was born from the desire to protect the landscapes that we all cherish for generations to come.

By purchasing this book you have helped save the open spaces that give context to our community. Thank you.

How You Can Help Save Land

Join Our 1% for Open Space Program

1% for Open Space allows local businesses to support the permanent protection of open space in Park City and Summit County by adding a small donation to their customers' purchases. The donation is always voluntary. In some cases, the donation is 1% of the purchase price, or a business may add $1 or 1% to a night's lodging fee. In some situations the business owner chooses to make the donation, rather than asking customers to contribute.

These donations add up to form a significant resource that the Summit Land Conservancy uses to protect local open space, trails, wildlife habitat, farms, ranches, and rivers.

The following businesses are members of our 1% for Open Space program:

- Cole Sport
- Copper Moose Farm
- Deer Valley Resort
- Heidi and Peter Gatch Real Estate
- Jans Mountain Outfitters/White Pine Touring
- Michael LaPay Real Estate
- Park City Lodging
- Park City Ski Places
- Peterson/Calder Real Estate
- Snow Flower Property Management
- Treasure Mountain Inn
- 350 Main Brasserie

Become a Member

Visit our website to join and to learn more about what we do. Together, we can save land! Visit **www.summitlandconservancy.org**.

Adopt an Easement

The Summit Land Conservancy relies on the help of volunteers to monitor our protected lands. Volunteers visit the property of their choice twice a month and report on the condition of the property. From hiking, biking, and nature walks to fishing and wildlife watching, our protected lands offer a variety of recreational activities that enable easy monitoring. You can make a valuable contribution by helping ensure that the terms of the conservation easements are met.

Summit Land Conservancy Protected Properties

Empire Canyon: Lady Morgan
1.79 acres, 2002

Empire Canyon: Prospect Ridge
64.75 acres, 2002

Empire Canyon: Ski Area
883 acres, 2002

Empire Canyon: Silver King
143 acres, 2002

Enclave at Cedar Draw
63.25 acres, 2006

Fawcett Ranch
43.53 acres, 2009

Judd Ranch
34.59 acres, 2011

McPolin Farmlands
115.57 acres, 2005

Miss Billie's
10.95 acres, 2012

Osguthorpe Ranch
121 acres, 2012

Quarry Mountain
183 acres, 2008

Rail Trail
1.97 acres, 2005

Richards Ranch
18.92 acres, 2005

Round Valley: Bilogio
143.7 acres, 2005

Round Valley: Cranbrook
40 acres, 2005

Round Valley: Ed Gillmor
186 acres, 2005

Round Valley: Grover
40 acres, 2005

Round Valley: McMillian
280 acres, 2005

UP&L on Main Street
0.51 acres, 2005

Virginia Mining Claims
13.3 acres, 2005

Warren Claims
105 acres, 2002

See maps on following pages.

Park City Area Easements 2012

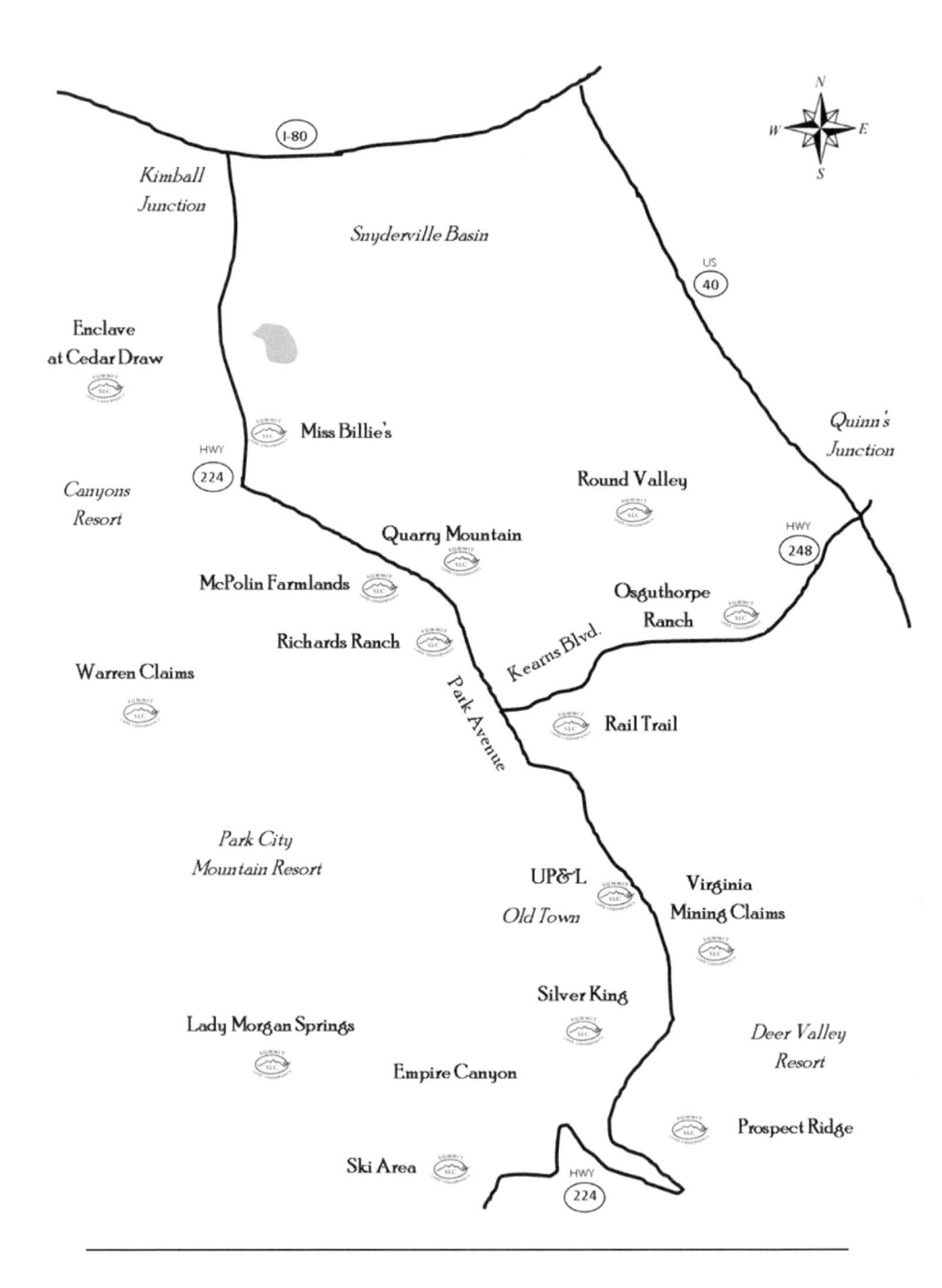

Weber River Watershed Easements 2012

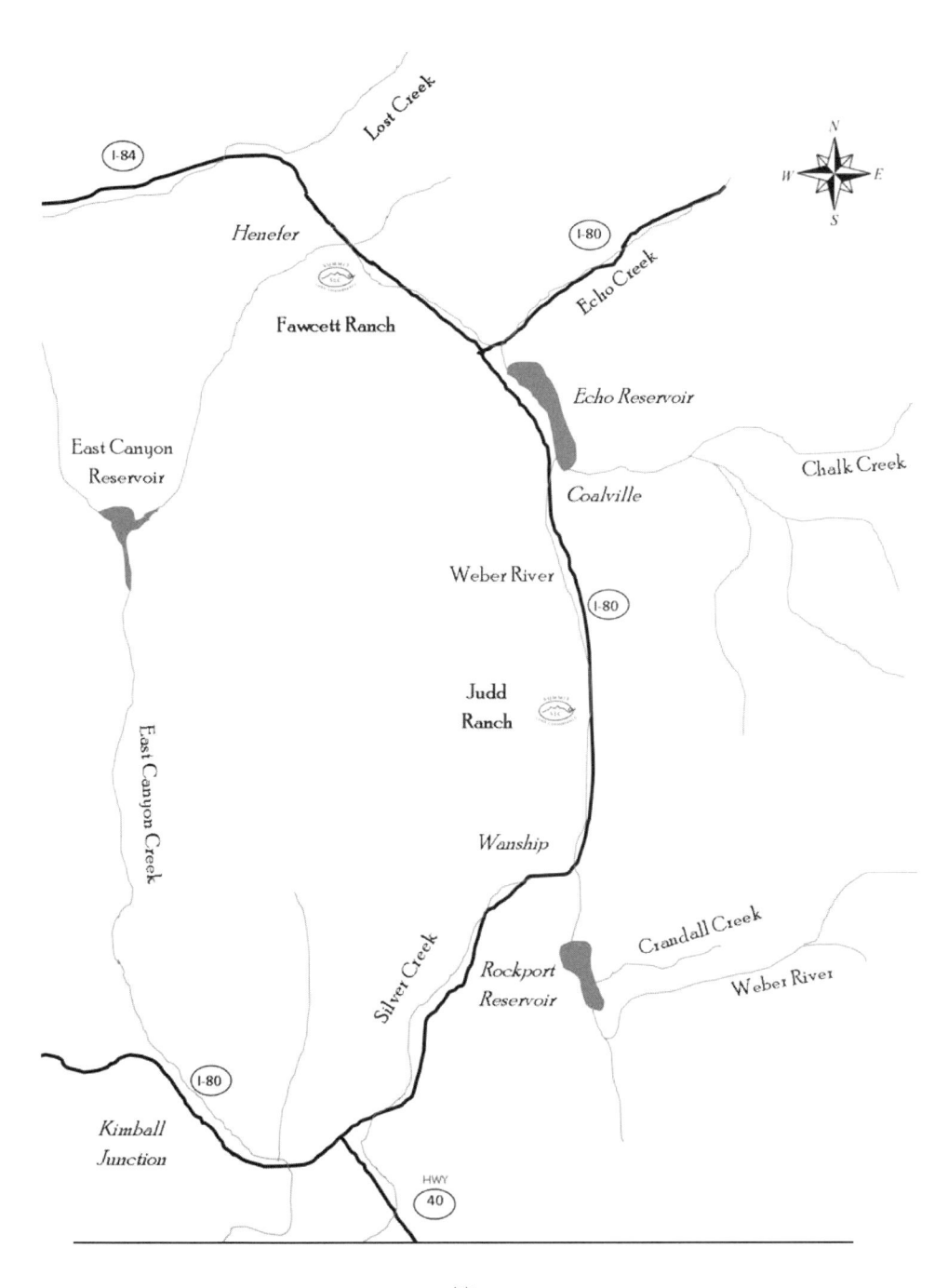

About the Artists

Stefania Barr is a 17 year-old photographer/artist, actor, and musician based in Summit County. In all of her artistic endeavors she strives to promote the preservation of the exceptional, to inspire change leading toward refinement, and to edify the human soul.

Robin Cornwell is a local artist with a studio/gallery in Park City. The beauty of Utah's nature is the inspiration for Robin's impressionistic landscapes. www.robincornwell.com

Sue Galusha has been a Park City High School art teacher for the past 14 years. When not at school, she can be found either skiing at PCMR or painting in oils, watercolors or encaustics. She loves all of it. Some of her work can be seen at www.art-exchange.com and at the Park City Professional Artists Association.

As a resident of Park City since 1990, **Renee Mox Hall** finds inspiration for her paintings in Summit County's pristine outdoors. Look for her on the Rail Trail and look for her artwork in local galleries and at www.yessy.com/reneemoxhall.

After graduating from Parson's School of Design in New York City, **John Helton** moved to Park City where he has been creating sculpture and fine art furniture in bronze, copper, and wood for over 25 years. His work can be seen in collections and exhibitions throughout the United States and also at www.johnhelton.com.

Alisa Livingston studied art at Park City High School and graduated with the class of 2012. Alisa was a student of fellow *Park City Witness* artist, Sue Galusha.

Letitia Lussier has been inspired by Park City's natural beauty since 1981, and as a life time artist she realizes the value of preserving the land. She is grateful for the opportunity to participate in this program. To see more of Letitia's work, please visit www.letitialussier.com.

Mark Maziarz has been photographing Park City for almost 23 years. He has recently discovered an affinity for how blur and imperfection can highlight and inform his work, just like life. www.ParkCityStock.com

Linda McCausland has been coming to Park City on vacation for over 30 years and has lived here for eight years. She likes painting the landscapes and wildlife that she finds while exploring the outdoors in the area. She likes painting en plein air as well as in her studio in several media. www.lindamccausland.com

Michael O'Malley's outdoor photography captures the beauty of the land that he tirelessly works to preserve in his role on the Board of Trustees of Summit Land Conservancy. Michael enjoys sharing his knowledge of Park City's mining history as a tour guide in Empire Canyon and Deer Valley. When he's not exploring the great outdoors, Michael is Marketing Director for the Utah Science Technology and Research (USTAR) Initiative and the Governor's Office of Economic Development.

Jan Perkins is a painter of rural landscapes, historic barns and farms. She paints horses, cows, and sheep as well as the occasional fly fishing scene. The rural valley where she lives has so much beauty that it could easily take more than a lifetime to capture. www.JanPerkins.com

Rick Pieros has been traveling the rural and wild areas of the western United States since his youth. Drawn to the remnants of the American West's rich and colorful past, Rick's current emphasis is abstract details of weathered detritus: miner's shacks, abandoned automobiles, mining equipment, etc. Rick owned and operated Wild Spirits Nature Photography studio on historic Main Street in Park City until 2007. He currently lives at the base of the Wasatch Mountains with his wife Heidi and two daughters, Hailey and Ivy. www.rickpieros.com

Virginia (Gincy) Carrington Plummer lives and works in Park City with her family and dogs. She owns Carrington Studios and chairs the Park City Professional Art Association Board. Gincy ventures into wide open spaces for the healing, exercise, and inspiration that the natural beauty around Summit County offers. www.carringtonstudios.com

Dori Pratt currently is celebrating 52 glorious years in Park City. When she is not on the slopes of Deer Valley or at the Park City Municipal golf course, you can find her in her studio making jewelry or painting. In her free time, she takes photos. www.parkcityart.com

Greg Ragland is both a painter and a sculptor currently residing in Park City. He received his BFA from Art Center College of Design and his MFA from the University of Utah. His current paintings of detailed birds in minimal abstracted color compositions are a contemporary take on a typically traditional subject matter. www.gregragland.com

Felix Saez is a self-taught, local artist-in-residence at his Stone Art Gallery on Main Street in Old Town Park City. He specializes in original paintings and relief sculptures of wildlife and American Indian images depicted on stone. www.fineartonstone.com

Allison Willingham is an award-winning oil painter and an honors graduate from The Massachusetts College of Art in Boston. She has been living in Park City for the past 23 years. Her images are reflections of the natural world and impressions of the western landscape. A thick, painterly brushstroke and vibrant color palette define her unique style. For this book, Allison chose an image of what a lavender farm could look like in Summit County, illustrating one way to preserve our open space through sustainable agriculture.

Acknowledgements

This book project was made possible by the generous contributions of the local writers and artists whose work is found in these pages.

The Conservancy extends its additional gratitude and karmic benefits to:

Editor *Jane Gendron* for her gentle and thoughtful editing,

Liz Craig Myers at Nine-Grain Design for her beautiful design work,

Terri Borg at Turnkey Publishing for her printing expertise,

Andy Beerman and *Thea Leonard* at Treasure Mountain Inn and the Lockwood Family Foundation for their generous support of this project,

Sue Fassett, Sally Tauber, Amy Roberts, Juli-Anne Warll, Rick Pieros, Celeste McMullin, and *Joe Totten* for their invaluable advice and support,

Dolly's Bookstore, the *Swaner EcoCenter Gift Shop,* and *Atticus Coffee, Books and Teahouse.*